LIFE IS A DASH

COPYRIGHT © 2019. ALL RIGHTS RESERVED.

No part of this publication may be reproduced, distributed, or transmitted in any form or by any means, including photocopying, recording, or other electronic or mechanical methods, or by any information storage and retrieval system without the prior written permission of the publisher, except in the case of very brief quotations embodied in critical reviews and certain other noncommercial uses permitted by copyright law.

We all know our date of birth. We don't know when we are going to leave this life on earth. If you look at a tombstone. You see a persons date of birth and that persons date of death.

In between those two dates is a dash. That dash represents that persons life on earth. While we are alive. We are living in our dash. In other words your life is a dash. This book was writen to show a person how to live in their DASH!!!!!!

We only have one life to live. This book will give definition of the age ole question; WHAT IS LIFE?

I will explain how to have a happy life, with purpose, the right mindset, being thankful and most of all. How to forgive and be humble.

When this is achieved. You will have lived a wonderful happy life. A life with purpose and and meaning. A life that will have caused changed in one's self and others.

This is a life that will live on forever and ever.

Even the DASH represents a persons life. You can have a live that will live much much longer than the dates on a tombstone..

Table of Contents

YOU ONLY ONCE

CHAPTER 1
WHAT IS LIFE

CHAPTER 2
TO BE HAPPY IS THE MEANING OF LIFE AND HAPPINESS IS ALREADY WITHIN US

CHAPTER 3
PURPOSE

CHAPTER 4
AMBITION - A QUALITY THAT CREATES A POSITIVE LIFE

CHAPTER 5
GET POSITIVE MINDSET FOR POSITIVE LIFE

CHAPTER 6
BEING THANKFUL

CHAPTER 7
DON'T COMPARE YOURSELF TO OTHERS

CHAPTER 8
FORGIVENESS AND POSITIVE LIVING

CHAPTER 9
HUMBLENESS

CHAPTER 10
PRAY

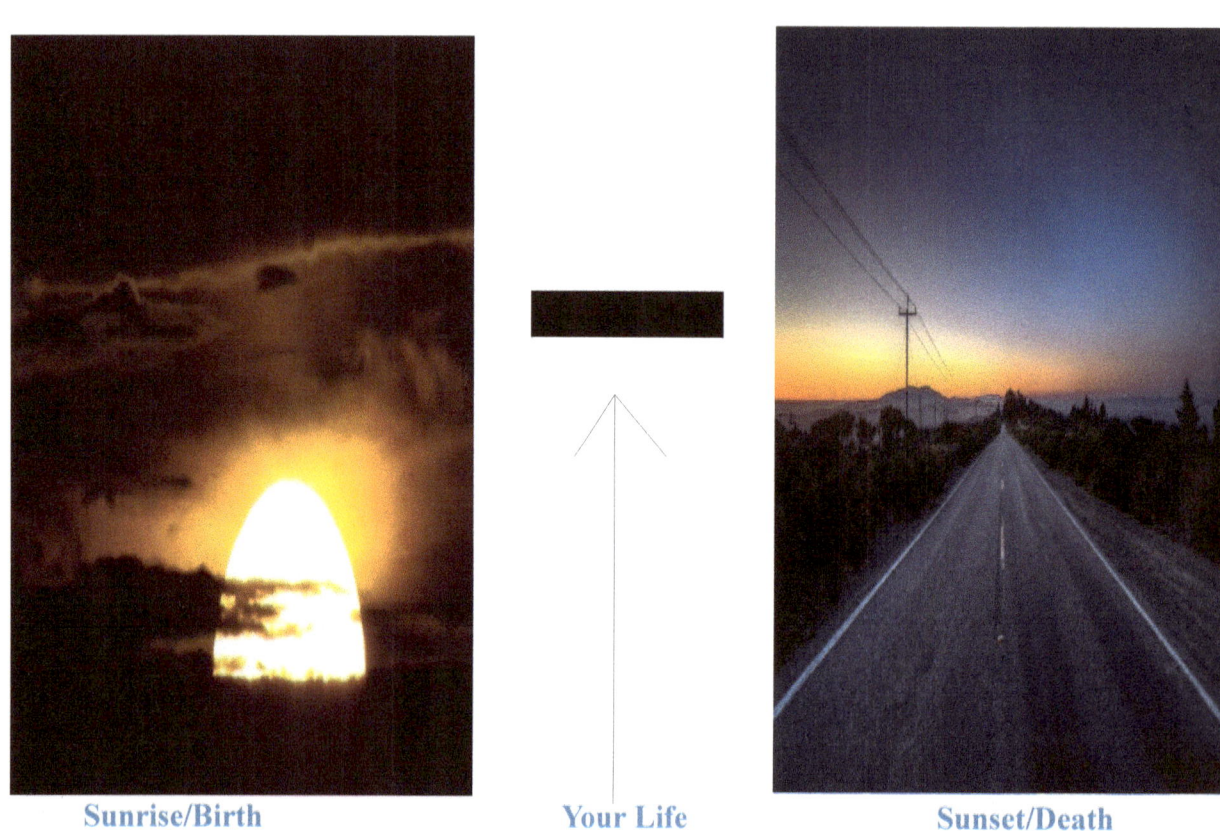

Sunrise/Birth   Your Life   Sunset/Death

LIFE IS A DASH

YOU ONLY LIVE ONCE

As the great actress, Mae West, once said, **"You only live once;** but if you do it right, once is enough."

This is very true in so many ways. You do, indeed only get to live once. This thought freaks out most people. A lot of people worry that they will never find their true happiness in life, or that they will never accomplish all they seek to accomplish.

But life is not a matter of accomplishing everything, rather it is a matter of living each day in a special way. Life is just a series of moments. Put a bunch of moments together and you have a day. Put seven days together and you have a week. Put 52 weeks together and you have a year. Put many years together and you have a lifetime. At the heart of all this, though, is that most basic unit: the moment.

You only live once, so your life is special. It is unique and precious. Once it is done, it is done. Furthermore, once each moment is done, it is done. You cannot get back your life, and you cannot get back your moments so you might as well make them count. In the end your legacy is all thats left.

By living each moment of life to its fullest potential you are doing all you can to show your gratitude to be alive. You are showing that you believe that life is important, and you value your time here on Earth.

Without life, you have nothing. Of course, you may have religious beliefs that state that there is more once life is over, but that is not the point of the book. The point is, that all you have <u>right now</u> is your life(**YOUR DASH**). Life is made up of moments of time. Therefore, the most important possession you have is time. Once your time is up, all that is left is your **LEGACY.**

Most of us waste a great deal of time in idleness. This means we are wasting precious units of life. It is one thing to waste a few bucks on a guilty pleasure; it is another thing entirely to waste time on nothingness.

You were put on this earth to **LIVE**, and that is true no matter what your religious beliefs are. You were not born to merely exist. You're not here to waste the precious gift of life. You are here to use each unit of life you can to create something special. Something that will last long after you have left this life.

Create something more valuable than was here previously. Add value to your life and the lives of those around you. Increase the value of the world to make it a better place for everyone to live. By doing this, you are creating more life. You are creating something very special.

You are treating life with respect. And for this, you will surely be rewarded. I don't know what your ultimate reward will be, but I do know that you will be rewarded in life with great happiness and satisfaction.

Spend each day by living each moment of life you have been given. Make each day value, and show your respect for life. Be grateful that you are here and have the opportunity to do great things. You may only live once, so do it **RIGHT!!!!!!!!!!**

CHAPTER 1

WHAT IS LIFE

Life by definition: **The period from birth to death.**

For the purposes for this book. This is the definition of life. Just know there are many definitions for the word

LIFE...

Life as Fun: Life in this context is viewed as pleasure; people with this mind-set centralize the whole of their living on getting pleasures from life. Nothing seems to be more important in life to them than having fun; from constant vacations, going to the movies, relaxations, partying, to everything which ultimately gives them pleasure.

People tend to be lackadaisical in everything they do, since life is all about fun there is no need to be serious minded. They tend to be restless too, because there is no lasting fulfillment in pleasure, it's only temporary, people with this view of life, are always in search of something new to do that will give them a higher degree of pleasure or fun. Their aim in life, is to enjoy all there is while alive and die having lived life to its "fullest".

There is nothing at all wrong with having fun. In fact your mind and body needs it. Just don't make having fun your main priorty. Having fun can also be when your helping others.

Life as a Journey: Looking at life from this perspective has a lot to do with the end. People, who view life from this angle, are not very ambitious, they are submissive to any circumstance that crosses their way in life, and they believe that life has a definite end for them which cannot be altered. Whichever direction life takes them is what has been ordained for them, if anything happens to them, be it good or bad, they never seem not to worry, if it had to happen at all, then it's their destiny - what fate has in stock for them. Life is a series of laid out events, events which they can neither question nor change. Although they believe in destiny, they never seek to find out their own destiny.

Their existence is based on the believe that, their life and whatever comes out of it, is guided by an infinite intelligence which eventually leads them to a happy ending. All they need do, is relax and enjoy the journey, everything is under control. They never take charge of their lives. Rather than take on the journey of life, they let life take them on a journey.

From the day we're born, we're on a life journey. There will be things we can't control which is a part of the jouney of life. But in most part we can control our life journey. If you dont contol where you're going, life will take you on a journey of destruction.

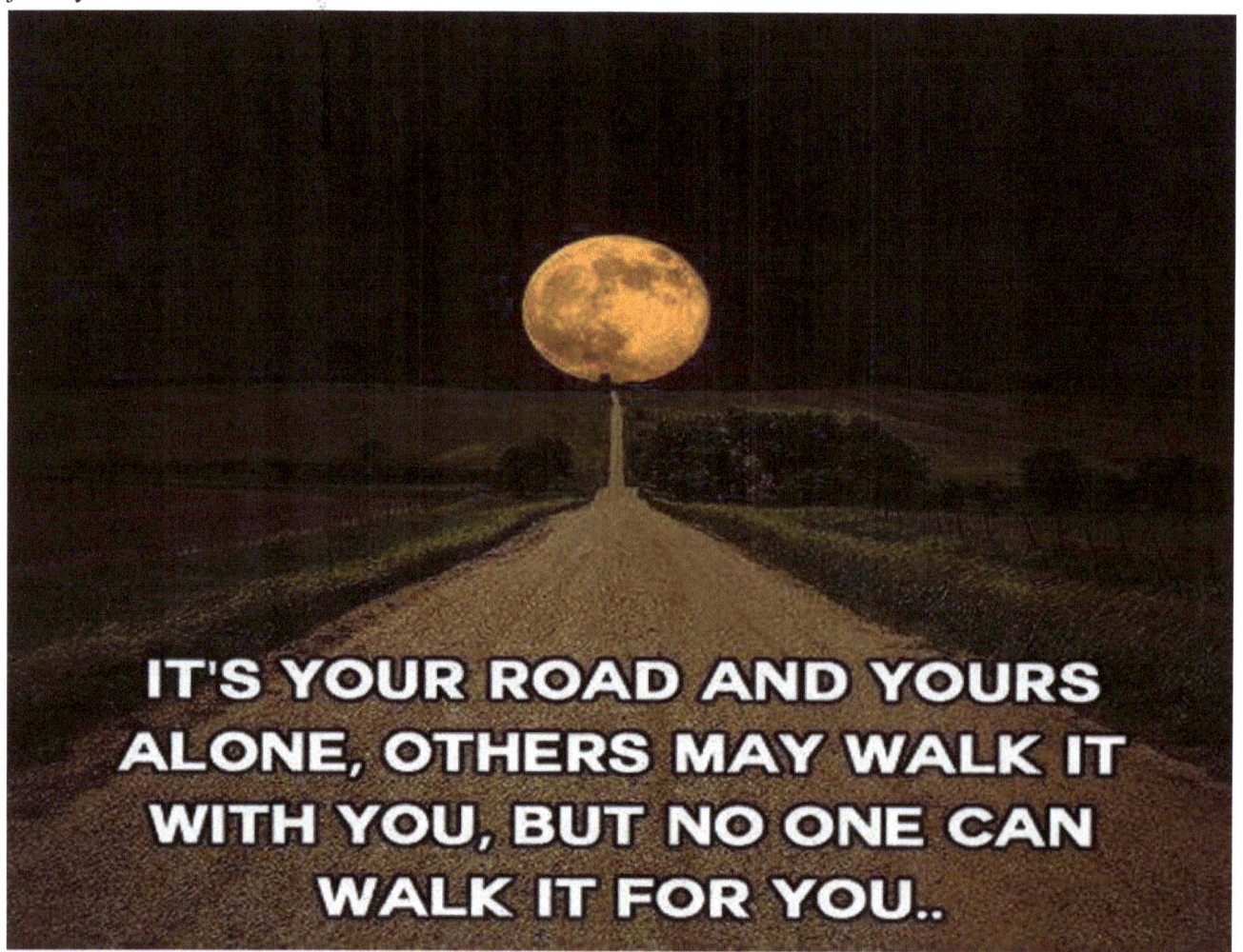

The lyrics to this song, sums it all up. Read these lyrics out loud to yourself..

Do You Know
Where you're going to?
Do you like the things?
That life is showing you
Where are you going to?
Do you know?

Do you get?
What you're hoping for?
When you look behind you
There's no open doors
What are you hoping for?
Do you know?

Once we were standing still, in time
Chasing the fantasies and feeling all nice
You knew how I loved you, but my-spirit was free
Laughing at the questions
That you once asked of me

Now looking back at all we've had
We let so many dreams just slip through our hands
Why must we wait so long, before we see?
How sad the answers to those questions can be

Do you get?
What you're hoping for
When you look behind you
There's no open doors
What are you hoping for?
Do you know?

Songwriters: Gerry Goffin / Michael Masser
Theme From Mahogany (Do You Know Where You're Going To)

Life as an Adventure: Unlike their counterparts who view life has a journey, people with this mind-set are more active and have ambitious. They're goal getters, always out to do something new, breaking new grounds and accomplishing great tasks. They're focused and persistent about what they have set out to accomplish. Life to them is all about achievements; life is just another exciting territory to explore.

They move from one thing to another, trying this and trying that, they are more like those seeking pleasures, always out for a greater task to accomplish. The difference being that, while they seek achievements, the fun lovers seek pleasures, by so doing they don't discover their true purpose on earth. In a bid to try and taste all there is, they sacrifice their true assignment for temporary fulfillments. At the end of their lives, there aim is to have written and passed a lot of test they alone have set for themselves. Life to them is an endless search.

When you find your true purpose in life. You won't have to search anymore. Then you can enjoy the many adventures, your purpose will bring.

Life as a Race: From the moment they are born, they deem themselves qualified for the race of life. They want to crawl, walk and talk all in one day. In all they do, they do in a rush, with the aim of making it first to the end. Often times, the means is sacrificed for the end; process is subordinated for result. Learning how its done is not their concern, getting it done is all that counts.

Life is measured in terms of speed. Who makes it first to the end? The finish line becomes the target and not the deeds; the number of lives or meaningful things one have accomplished. Their main focus is to get in the race, reach the finish line which ever way; right or wrong. Whether it's the right race, the right way or track is irrelevant to them. A life viewed from this perspective, is one that is filled with irregularities.

It's like a child who would not wait to be taught, who goes ahead to sit for the test, what else can you expect if not a failure? It's only normal because that which is skipped or short cut later re-surfaces and demands the due process of time. Life is not automatic. Speed isn't everything. In fact, it's worse than nothing if it moves you in the wrong direction faster and cheats you out of some of the best moments of the journey.

To have a meaningful life, it takes a conscious and continuous effort and patience. You can't cut corners and expect to have a full life, in the end; your life will be cut short. Unless you're headed in the right direction, increasing your speed will only get you to the wrong place faster. In addition, you'll miss many of the rich, satisfying moments of living along the way.

CHAPTER 2

TO BE HAPPY IS THE MEANING OF LIFE AND HAPPINESS IS ALREADY WITHIN US

Happiness is already within you. And to be happy is the meaning of life. At the same time, this concept is awkward in helping people to make it their own. But once it is grasped, it seems very easy to know.

What is Happiness?

Everyone wants to be happy. Everyone has experienced happiness at different times in their lives and knows what it feels like to be happy. It is an emotion to be strived for. But what is happiness?

Each person's definition of happiness is different. Each individual has an idea of what they feel they need in order to be happy. However, there are others who have everything they need in life but are still unhappy. So money don't make a person happy. Rich people wouldn't kill themselves if it did.

A happy person enjoys life. They are a magnet drawing others in and are pleasant to be around. They have a contagious smile. They most often have something nice to say or a helping hand to offer. A happy person carries a positive psychology, encouraging others around. Their lives are a reflection of goodness.

True happiness comes from within. It is how we feel about ourselves. It is not conditional, based on money, status, or materialistic possessions. Happiness is something we all choose to experience. It is feeling of contentment and joy that titillates the body from within and exudes to the outside.

You don't need to wait for some event to take place in your life to find happiness. Finding true happiness begins with gaining control over your thoughts. Remember, your thoughts ultimately decide your actions. By changing the way you think you can make you happier than you've ever been in your life. Your negative thoughts attract negative emotions and unhappiness. Your positive thoughts attract positive emotions and happiness. This is known as law of attraction.

The Comparison Trap Repels Happiness.

As humans, we place conditions on our happiness. We carry the thought that when we have achieved _____ we will be happy. Then we finally get what we want but the happiness is short-lived. You compare your life and circumstances with others and in no time you feel unhappy again. This is a trap we are all guilty of. Happiness runs away from this kind of mentality. It is a common trap and one we must stay clear of it.

Happiness is contentment! If you are content with your life each step of the way, you will achieve happiness each day of your life. True you have your ambitions and goals you aspire to. You may want more money, a better job, or a nicer house. But does that mean you have to wait until you have achieved these things in order to be happy? **No!!!!!!!!**

When working to achieve your goals in life, you must be able to enjoy your efforts and hard work each step of the way and find the happiness within. However, if you perpetually compare yourselves to others and what they have achieved you will never be able to find the happiness in whatever you do. Your efforts will always seem futile. You will feel as if you are making little progress. You will become dejected and unhappiness sets in.

If this is your strategy in life, you will very seldom find happiness because as soon as you have achieved one goal, there will be someone else you can find to compare your life with. It will be impossible to find anything meaningful in what you do. You lose patience and become desperate to find that instant gratification.

Remember, success is a journey. Nothing happens overnight. So enjoy each step of the way and find happiness in each stride of the journey.

If you are truly in the pursuit of happiness, you have to remove the conditions you place on your happiness. You have to avoid the comparison trap. You must begin to see your life in an optimistic light. You must give yourself credit for your efforts. And if you feel your efforts are not gaining ground, seek some direction. We all need assistance from time to time to get us back on target.

Happiness is a Choice.

True, many of us genetically carry a happy disposition. But even the happiest of persons experience sad days. The good news is that we can choose how happy we want to be.

When you feel unhappy, you automatically assume it is due to a lack of something. You immediately begin to desire material things hoping it will fill that void that you feel. Maybe it's a new car, or a new house, or a new job. You begin to anticipate these things, waiting for your happiness to arrive. When the quick fixes don't arrive the unhappiness still exists.

The root of the problem stems from a distorted self-perception. The perception you carry of yourself can sabotage any chance you have of happiness. The first step in choosing a life of happiness begins by changing your self-concept.

You must believe you can be happy at whatever stage of life's journey you are at. I read about a man who suffered a stroke at 37, it was a very trying period of nis life that made him feel very fearful and sad. The recuperation from brain surgery left him feeling helpless and unhappy. He didn't know how long my recuperation process would last but he realized he had to do something to bring some joy and happiness back into his life.

He made the decision to work with the impoverished, helping to restore a clinic that was destroyed in an earthquake. His happiness was instantly restored. He felt happy for life and living. He recognized that happiness is a choice and He chose to do something to bring back some joy and happiness to his life. He felt happy for each breath he was able to take. He gave thanks each day for the chance to awake to see his family.

You too can claim your happiness. You too can make that decision to find happiness in your life. No one expects you to be perfect. You are the one that hold yourself to perfection. Find ways to restore peace and joy in your life and observe how much more success you will achieve. Events in your life will flow smoother, relationships will be more meaningful and life will be sweeter.

The sooner you accept that happiness is a choice, and that you can choose to be happy, the sooner you will begin to feel happiness flowing through you. Make that choice today!

How to Choose Happiness.

Choosing to be happy is being able to recognize the simple things in life that we can derive happiness from. I am providing this list in hopes that you can look inside your life and recognize the happiness that already exists and how you can bring it out or how to bring more happiness into your life. Here's how you can choose to be happy.

Having good health - Don't take your good health for granted. Be happy for the blessings of good health and be good to your body, don't abuse it. Moderation is the key.

The friends in your life - Cherish the friendships in your life and the happiness they bring. Don't take your friends for granted. Invite them over for a dinner party or barbeque. Let them see how appreciative you are for having them in your life.

Family - Strengthen the family bonds you have. Your family can bring a lot of happiness to your life. If the bonds are broken, work on mending them.

Meditation - This is a technique you can use to remove the unnecessary clutter and negativity from your thoughts that can cloud your ability to recognize happiness in your life. Clear the cobwebs and learn to think clearly again.

Biofeedback- If you have difficulty in choosing your thoughts, this is a technique you can use to bring more positive thinking in your life. Remember controlling your thoughts and removing negativity can bring you instant happiness.

Feed your spiritual void - When we are spiritually full, we are transcended into another realm of thinking. We discover ways of finding more meaning and happiness in our lives more easily. We dwell on positive things and discard ugly habits such as judgmentalism, criticism, cynicism, bitterness, and strife. These things harbor unhappiness within.

Have a sense of direction - We must have projects, work, something to feel productive about in our lives, or a set of goals that we aspire to. This brings happiness into our lives. The feeling of nonproductivity leaves one feeling useless and unhappy.

Find an emotional connection - Having a meaningful relationship with another person can bring a lot of happiness to our lives. We are social creatures that need to be with others and not always alone. Loneliness breeds unhappiness. To love and be loved is happiness in a bottle.

Avoid conflict - One way to remain happy is to maintain good relationships with people. Whether it is with a coworker, a friend, a family member, or the cashier at the grocery store. When you are hostile to others it has a way of coming back to you like a boomerang. Be patient with the people you encounter and be good to your fellowman. This will bring peace and happiness into your life.

Do for others - When you do kind acts for others it bounces back to you in the form of joy and happiness. No matter how small, go out of your way to do something nice for someone. It pays big happiness dividends.

Be thankful each day - When you wake up each morning give thanks for the wonderful things in your life. Send those sentiments of gratitude out to God or to the universe and watch how much happier you feel throughout your day. We have a tendency as humans to dwell on the negative and see the glass as half empty rather than half full. By giving thanks for all the blessings in your life, big or small, you are allowing more room for happiness to reside.

CHAPTER 3

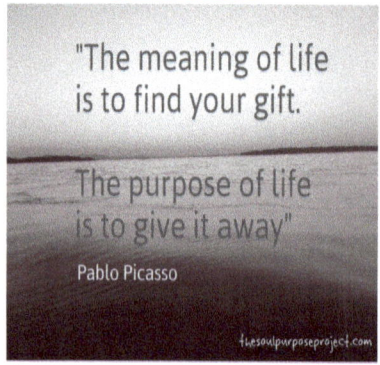

PURPOSE

When we talk about purpose, we are talking about our reason for being and for doing. Life is meaningless without knowing and living out our purpose. Some people will commit suicide because they feel that their life has no purpose, and without purpose there is no hope. God created man in His image and gave him a purpose that included spiritual fellowship and productive service. A purpose isn't simply an ideal; it's something that we have strong convictions about: we believe in it and it informs our actions.

Purpose generates excitement - An excitement that enables us to leap over every obstacle. It helps us to develop tenacity. I become excited when I know what God wants me to accomplish, when I know why I'm here and when I understand the possibilities of my future. I develop endurance, that can't quit attitude that allows me to rise above challenges. Don't get me wrong - purpose doesn't minimize or even eliminate challenges. It just helps me to have the drive to succeed in spite of them.

A true purpose is God given: It requires sensitivity and listening to God's voice. To know our purpose and to maximize that purpose, we need to develop an intimate relationship with the Lord through the Holy Spirit. Developing that relationship involves prayer and studying and meditating on the Word of God. The faith chapter in Hebrews 11 tells us about numerous people who realized their purpose because of their faith in God. Noah, through his faith, realized his purpose of saving his family and humanity from extinction. Abraham realized his purpose of being a blessing to the nations and becoming a father of faith for billions of people.

Moses realized his purpose of being a deliverer for the Israelites rescuing them from their Egyptian captivity.

Every truly spiritual/mature believer has a sense of purpose. All believers have purpose but not all believers know their purpose because they have not developed that sensitivity to God's voice.

Purpose motivates us and we motivate and mobilize others. When we understand and embrace our purpose, we become excited and there is a willingness to get up and go. We know what we are about. Purpose as the 'why' helps us to figure out the 'what' and the 'how.'

Having motivation then leads to motivating and mobilizing others. This is particularly true of leaders. Strong leaders know their purpose: they know what they have to do, where they have to go and who they have to recruit. Leaders know that they can't accomplish their purpose alone. They need to bring people along with them. Some of those persons will come to recognize their purpose and may eventually branch out. A person who lacks motivation is a person who lacks purpose.

Purpose motivates diligence. When we are strongly committed to our purpose, we will be motivated to work hard. We understand that hard work is needed in order to be successful. Someone has quipped that the only place success comes before work is in the dictionary. When we are driven by our purpose, we will make needed sacrifices. At times, we will put in long hours because that is what is required to fulfill our purpose. However, working hard does not mean that we have to compromise on those things that are important such as our relationship with God and our relationship to our family. The difference between a dreamer and a visionary is effort. A dreamer can conceptualize but doesn't invest the effort to actualize. The visionary sees the possibilities and actively takes the steps to ensure that they are turned into realities.

Purpose causes leaders to prioritize. Leaders can't accomplish everything; similarly, they cannot meet all expectations. Leaders must focus on those activities that actualize their purpose. Activities can be divided into urgent but not important, important but not urgent, neither urgent nor important, both urgent and important. Leaders must determine which category an activity falls into. This means that some things must be left undone. Leaders must recognize that not all positions and jobs help them to realize their purpose. Some things require leaders' attention but are minor; these should not be time consuming. Leaders must invest time in the major activities; some things can be delegated - e.g. the apostles left the waiting on tables to the deacons. Leaders who try to do everything not only fail to realize their purpose but are also candidates for burnout. Jesus is a great example of maintaining one's priorities. He came to do the will of His Father and He did not deviate from that purpose.

Purpose keeps us grounded in the present as opposed to the past while preparing for the future. It keeps us focused on what needs to happen now. It keeps us grounded in reality rather than dreaming about the future. Purpose helps us to overcome the monotony of life: life is not a string of exhilarating activities. In today's culture of instant gratification, people are looking for excitement, so they abandon things that are no longer thrilling. Persons who have purpose will stick to their task until the goal is realized. Purpose reminds us that we're going somewhere - activities add up. The journey may be long, but we know we are making progress with every step we take.

Know your purpose, maximize your potential. Giftedness alone is not sufficient; without purpose even a gifted person will fail to realize his potential. When we have purpose we will look for opportunities to actualize that purpose. Purpose challenges us to overcome our deficiencies and fears.

Purpose causes us to improve through studying and practice. Purpose leads to creativity; it helps us to find the resources that are needed.

Is your purpose being realized? If not. **Why**?_____

Are you accomplishing what you set out to do? If not. **Why**?_____

Remember. If you want something bad enough. You'll do whatever it takes to aquire what you want.

what do you want to do in your life?

CHAPTER 4

AMBITION - A QUALITY THAT CREATES A POSITIVE LIFE

Ambition; is a word that is used to describe the characteristic of people who go out and get what they want in life. They are the ones who learn how to bloom where they are planted. They are the ones who find a way to get to top in life, even if they start at the bottom. Though ambitious people are sometimes painted in a bad light, because of the intensity that they often bring to the table with everything they do, they possess a trait that is a valuable component of good personal development.

To lead a positive life you have to be happy, and, to be happy, most people need to have goals and a purpose for their life. Usually, people who stop having goals and desires become depressed and sedentary. Without dreams, goals, and the ambition to get there we start to lose a part of our humanity. You might have everything you need in life, but you won't feel the positive rush of adrenaline that we all get when we conquer something that we've wanted to do for years, such as graduating from college or getting a good job.

Without ambition it is difficult to truly achieve satisfactory personal development success. You can't succeed without this trait because it is the driving force behind what brings personal success. The truth is that this isn't some magical characteristic that only certain, powerful people possess. It is something that is in us all. We just have to figure out what it is that we want bad enough to bring it out and develop our ambition.

If you want to stoke your own drive to succeed, think about all the things in your life that are important to you. Make a list of those things and take some time to meditate on what you have come up with. It may be a hobby, a business that you would like to start, a career you hope to have one day, a new house or maybe to have children. Whatever it is, if there is something on that list that you want bad enough, then go for it. That feeling, that burning in your soul to do better, that's your ambition talking.

Though it might not, at first, be clear how you can go about getting the thing you want, you will eventually figure it out if you make it a priority. Small steps often lead to big accomplishments and you'd be surprised where some people started their journey toward the great things that they do today. For example, if you want to go to college one day, start by filling in the Financial Aid Form and see what you can get.

For those who are interested in travelling, begin saving up a few dollars every week and you will find that it can grow. If you want to be a teacher you could start by volunteering at area day-cares to get experience with children.

Pretty soon you'll start to run on ambition. The amount of personal development that you can undergo in just a short time is incredible. Before you know it, you will be leading a much more positive life, probably doing something that you love and that you never thought possible before.

CHAPTER 5

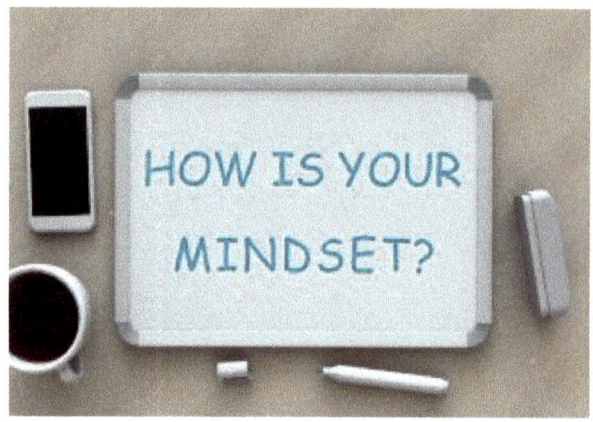

GET POSITIVE MINDSET FOR POSITIVE LIFE

Get Positive Mindset For Positive Life. Our mindset is the one thing that's the determining factor in relation to being successful in any area of life. You have to watch out not to let destructive ideas or attitudes hold you again or make you're feeling inadequate. Those kind of thoughts can and can preserve you proper where you are, never letting you reach your potential. A positive mindset alternatively will put you exactly the place you wish to be.

The suitable angle will open doors of alternative which have all the time seem to have been locked. A positive attitude will raise you up and energize you. It will give you confidence that can show in the whole lot you do, regardless of how small. That can-do perspective provides you with what you want to get that promotion you've got been wanting at your job, or allow you to make that presentation a success! Possibly you want to begin a business however are afraid to take that leap. That is the destructive mindset holding you back. You'll never strive something with those ideas in control! You'll be able to have your individual successful business.

There are plenty of profitable business homeowners out there. Some are in all probability your neighbors! For those who talk to them, I wager you'd discover that they are positive thinkers who don't dwell on the damaging things. That's to not say they do not generally fear, but the positive thinker will at all times see it by way of and find a way. Not like the adverse thinker who would just give up and blame it on their scenario or on society or something other than themselves. It is easier to do that than attempt to change. Really its not simpler! It takes loads of power to provide you with all those excuses and have to elucidate to everyone why you failed. All you need is to get Positive Mindset for Positive Life

Changing your mindset may be as easy as telling your self you can do it. Just tell yourself everyday and sometimes in the course of the day that you're OK and you are good sufficient and you will succeed at that enterprise or that dream or goal you have! Self-affirmation generally is a powerful technique for change.

You have to lift yourself up and consider in yourself and know that you can do anything you set your mind to! Do not consider that assertion as being boastful or bragging, it is just that it's important to elevate yourself up and not watch for another person to do it for you. Simply strive it and see for yourself that in case you are according to it, in no time at all you may see an enormous change in yourself for the higher in your attitude, mood and confidence levels. You will be in your technique to reaching something in life that you want!

GET POSITIVE MINDSET FOR POSITIVE LIFE

CHAPTER 6

BEING THANKFUL

When you read the many articles and advertisements about how to tap into the way to abundance, do you ever wish you were someone else - just sometimes? Like maybe a super salesman personality, the confident type who quietly presses all the right buttons to get almost everyone to buy? Do you envy the confidant entrepreneur who does not (seemingly) have the nervous reactions you get when your sale or proposal is rejected or criticised? Being thankful truly puts us in a different vibrational mode. To start where we are, without longing for or experiencing angst over who or where we should be, being thankful brings us to this exact present moment.

Be thankful right now, take stock of your abundances. Your home, your money, your untapped potential. But how to tap into that potential? Your goals and dreams and imagined outcomes that sometimes feel real, and feel altogether **YOU.** These desired results are often surrounded by barbed wire tipped emotional reactions and nervous responses, blocking your participation in your own daydreams!

Having the power and knowledge to bridge the gap between what you want to feel about your untapped potential and what you really DO feel about it - doubt, nervous reactions, and worse, is attainable. The nervous system has actual gateways - tiny points on our surfaces, that can be stimulated to reverse a nervous response to something. An allergen, an idea. A negative thought! The one that takes over, that you suppress and "out-think" with positive affirmations.

Positive self-talk works. But it feels futile if it prompts its exact opposite. Ever have that happen? In situations that demand high performance, sales ability, or influence over others, we may feel that we fall short. Yet these areas of function are the highly paid works in our society. Fine tuning the mechanisms of manifestation, means simply vibrating with your dreams, regardless of what you actually do. But that habitual nagging doubt undermines your frequency.

But there is help! There are ways to reverse your negative responses to an idea, an ambition, a desired outcome. The body is made to be accessed, to make your system work for you.

Try these 7 ways to manage (and decrease) your negative thoughts:

1. Recognize thought distortions. Our minds have clever and persistent ways of convincing us of something that isn't really true. These inaccurate thoughts reinforce negative thinking. If you can recognize them, you can learn to challenge them. Here are four common thought distortions:

- *Black and white thinking.* Seeing everything as one way or another, without any in between.
- *Personalizing.* Assuming you are to blame for anything that goes wrong, like thinking someone did not smile at you because you did something to upset her. (It's more likely that person is having a hard day and her mood had nothing to do with you.)
- *Filter thinking.* Choosing to see only the negative side of a situation.
- *Catastrophizing.* Assuming the worst possible outcome is going to happen.

2, Challenge negative thoughts. Whenever you have a distorted thought, stop and evaluate whether it is accurate. Think about how you would respond if a friend spoke about herself that way. You would probably offer a good rebuttal to his or her negative view. Apply the same logic to your own thoughts. Ask yourself if you are assuming the worst will happen or blaming yourself for something that has not gone the way you wanted. And then think about other possible outcomes or reasons that something turned out differently than you hoped.

3. Take a break from negative thoughts. It is possible to learn how to separate from negative thoughts. One way to do this is to allow yourself a certain amount of time (maybe five minutes) with the thought. Then take a break from focusing on it and move on with your day.

4. Release judgment. We all judge ourselves and others, usually unconsciously. Constantly comparing ourselves to other people or comparing our lives to some ideal breeds dissatisfaction. When you are able to let go of judgment (not easy, but possible), you will likely feel more at ease. Some ways to take a break from judgmental thoughts include recognizing your own reaction, observing it, and then letting it go. Another helpful technique is to "positive judge." When you notice you are negatively judging a person, yourself, or a situation, look for a positive quality, too.

5. Practice graditude. Research shows that feeling grateful has a big impact on your levels of positivity and happiness. Even when you are experiencing a challenging time in your life, you can usually find things (even small things) to be grateful for. Noticing the things that are going well and making you feel happy will keep you in touch with them. Keeping a gratitude journal and writing a few things in it every day is one easy and effective way to do this.

6. Focus on your strengths. It's human nature to dwell on the negative and overlook the positive. The more you can practice focusing on your strengths and not dwelling on mistakes you've made, the easier it will be to feel positive about yourself and the direction your life is taking. If you find yourself thinking harsh thoughts about your personality or actions, take a moment to stop and think about something you like about yourself.

7. Seek out professional support. If you are unable to manage your thoughts or find they are interfering with your ability to meet your daily responsibilities or enjoy life. Counseling and therapycan help you weather life changes, reduce emotional suffering and experience self-growth.

CHAPTER 7

DON'T COMPARE YOURSELF TO OTHERS

Don't Compare Yourself With Anyone In This World.. If You Do So, You Are Insulting Yourself - Bill Gates

It is true we are not alone in this world. There are billions of people living around us, some of which is our familiar and rest is strangers. It's also a fact that we cannot live on our own, we need to keep pace with people's lives. Competition and win have become the purpose of life. You want to lead the world and to beat your competitors to prove yourself ahead of all. Well, it's a good thing because you get success in this spirit. Until then, it's good as long as you have achieved success.

But take heed, the spirit is not the only cause of success. Luck, Environment, Resource, and Experience also counts, and in all these things we have no control. Hence neither you should compare yourself to someone else nor need to feel pain after losing. God has sent us for different purposes with distinct destiny, talent, strength, resource and nature. You cannot compare yourself to others but can take inspiration. We all have different journey so it's worthless to compare.

Here's a little story that shows why we should not compare ourselves to anyone else:

Tom and Harry are good friends who both study in the same class. Tom is blessed with a big family whereas Harry is an orphan. One side Harry lives alone and need to handle all responsibility besides studies and on the other side, Tom is free from all responsibility and need to only focus on his studies. In a day of 24 hours, Tom is just focus on studies and that's why he earns better marks than Harry, but Harry also has to take care of things like maintenance of the house, financial management, food, personal life and so many things plus studies.

Tom is blessed with an affection of his family, love, support, and he's mentally free, but, unfortunately, Harry is unlucky in these cases. One day Harry tries to just focus on studies by leaving all other work and he succeeds. Harry gets more marks than Tom in the examination. He achieves this milestone but still feels unhappy because he was hungry of his parent's love and support not marks. He could earn good marks because it is up to the spirit, but cannot find the love of his parents because it is up to the destiny.

Do you think Harry should compare with his friend Tom in terms of love from the parents? Absolutely not! Well, this is just an example for understanding why it is wrong to compare yourself to someone else. Anything can happen in the future because somewhere life is based on your luck. But you must remember to not compare yourself to anyone else.

Never!!!!!

"Personality begins where comparison leaves off. Be unique. Be memorable. Be confident. Be proud." ~Shannon L. Alder

You know it already.

You know you shouldn't compare yourself to others. Yet, that's often easier said than done.

Job title, income, grades, house, and Facebook likes—the number of categories in which we can compare ourselves to others are infinite. So is the number of people we can compare ourselves to.

Comparison is generally the fast track to unhappiness. It's a recipe for misery. All it does is keeping you focused on what you don't like about yourself and your life.

Ever since I made the decision to change careers, I've tried to focus on my new path. I've pictured myself as a horse with blinders, because I knew that looking too much on the sides would only keep me side-tracked.

It worked for a while. While I was out traveling for a year I kept my eyes on the prize, so to speak. But, when I came back home again, it wasn't so easy anymore.

I caught myself glancing over to what other people had, and I didn't. Where they were in life and I wasn't. I had made the decision to rebuild my life from scratch, so of course, I was "behind" when comparing myself to my friends.

The more I focused on their path, and not my own, the more I lost control. Eventually, I reached a point where I questioned my decision, and that's when I knew I had to change perspective quickly.

Here are thirteen simple ways to stop comparing yourself to others:

1. Water your own grass.

When we focus on other people, we lose time that we could otherwise invest in ourselves. We don't grow green grass by focusing on our neighbor's garden, we do it nurturing our own. So, instead of wasting time comparing your path to someone else's, spend it investing, creating, and caring for your own.

2. Accept where you are.

You can't change something you don't acknowledge. So, instead of resisting or fighting where you are, come to peace with it. Say yes to every part of your life, and from that place, make decisions that will move you in the right direction.

3. Love your past.

Your life might have been messy and bumpy. It might have been colored by mistakes, anxiety, and fear. I know mine has. But all those things were catalysts to help you become a better, wiser, and more courageous version of yourself. So, embrace your story and how much you've grown from it. Be proud of what you've done and for wanting to create a better life for yourself.

4. Do a social media detox.

We're constantly bombarded with people who live #blessed lives on Instagram, Twitter, and Facebook. What we don't consider is that we often compare our own worst moments with someone else's highlight.

Social media can be a great source for inspiration. But, if it triggers inadequacy, self-doubt, and frustration, then choose to do a detox. Make sure you control social media and not the other way around.

5. Know that this isn't the end of the movie.

If you're not happy where you are today, remember that this is just a snapshot of your life. Where you are today doesn't say anything about where you'll be in one or three years from now. What matters isn't where you are. What matters is your mindset, attitude, and where you're going.

6. Be grateful for what you have.

Oprah said, "Be thankful for what you have; you'll end up having more. If you concentrate on what you don't have, you will never, ever have enough."

Whenever you find yourself looking at what other people have, remind yourself of what you're grateful for. For me, that means appreciating my family, my wonderful friends, and the fact that I'm living in a peaceful country (Sweden). So, shift focus from what you don't have, to what you do have.

7. Decide not to let fear guide your choices.

The choices we make are either based on love or fear. For example, I moved to Paris for a job I was really excited about. That was based on love. Then I stayed a bit too long because I was afraid of what would happen if I quit. That was based on fear.

I've made all my fear-based decisions out of insecurity and a feeling of scarcity. They've never taken me in the direction I wanted.

Make sure love is the foundation for your choices. To stay on track, ask yourself this powerful question, "What would love do right now?"

8. Realize that you're not perfect.

There will always be someone who's richer, smarter, and more attractive than you. No one is perfect. Trying to be perfect is not the solution. So, instead of getting down on yourself for your flaws, quirks, and imperfections, accept them fully. Free yourself by embracing the fact that you're perfectly imperfect.

9. Be your own ally.

That mean voice inside your head can tell you all kind of BS. Mine has told me that I'm boring, stupid, and ugly in comparison to others (and a bunch of other awful things).

Instead of joining in when the mean voice of comparison pops up, choose to be on your side. Relieve, soothe, and comfort yourself. Give yourself regular pep talks, and if you wouldn't say it to a friend, don't say it to yourself.

10. Turn comparison into inspiration.

We tend to compare our behind-the-scenes with someone else's big moment. We tend to focus on their success, not on the thousands of hours they've spent preparing and working for their achievement. Instead of letting other people's triumphs be a time to get down on yourself, let it be a door opener to possibilities. Let it be an inspiration for what you can be, do and have in life.

11. Stop "shoulding" yourself.

Comparison often leads to us "shoulding" all over ourselves. We say things such as, "I should have this by now" or "I should have come further." But statements like that just keep us focused on what we're lacking.

Instead of using "should" when expressing commitments, use "want" and notice how your inner dialogue shifts.

12. Compare yourself with you.

If you need to compare yourself with someone, compare yourself with you. What can you do to improve your life quality? How can you be a better and more loving person? How can you be nicer to yourself than you were yesterday? You are the only person you can compare yourself with.

13. Tell a better story.

If the story you're telling yourself isn't one of empowerment, strength, and optimism, then tell a better story.

Instead of telling yourself you're not competent enough to do the work you want to do, tell yourself you're brave enough to try something new. Instead of blaming yourself for mistakes in the past, remind yourself that you did the best you could and that you've learned from it.

Take Back What Belongs to You

Comparing ourselves to others often leaves us feeling frustrated, anxious, and paralyzed about moving forward. It doesn't help one single bit in creating the life we want. Instead, it just takes away valuable time and energy that could have been spent on building our future.

Whenever you focus on what other people have that you don't, you give away your power. Every minute spent on comparing your path to someone else's is a minute lost on creating your own.

So, take back your power from all the people, places, and situations where you've left it and bring it back home. Decide that your energy will be used for believing, not doubting, and for creating, not destroying.

Focus on you. Focus on watering your grass and building your path. Focus on being the best that you can be and share that with the rest of us.-Maria Stenvinkel

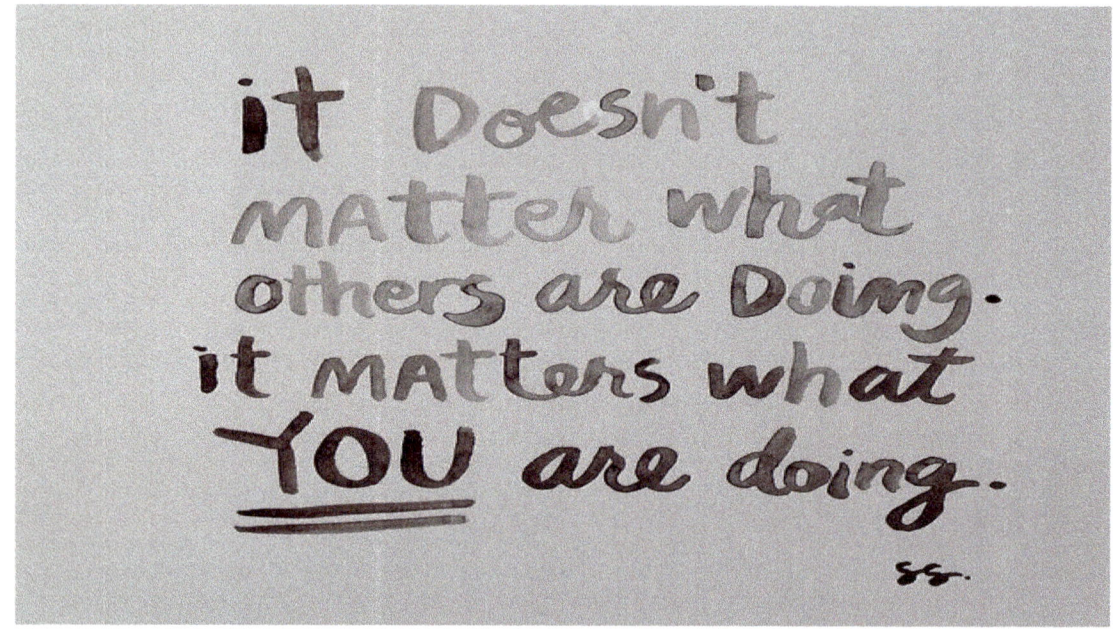

CHAPTER 8

FORGIVENESS AND POSITIVE LIVING

"Forgiveness is the key that can unshackle us from a past that will not rest in the grave of things over and done with. As long as our minds are captive to the memory of having been wronged, they are not free to wish for reconciliation with the one who wronged us.

Lewis B. Smedes.

Story of unknown author.

For over 20 years I carried a grudge, an anger closer to hatred of my own mother. I felt totally justified and was utterly convinced I had the right to express openly this anger against what I believed was my mother's absence and lack of caring, love or any motherly feelings toward me since the death of my father. In fact I drew my strength from these things to carry on with my life. Only a few close friends knew about it and even when I started doing my relaxation studies I never thought this issue had anything to do with my search for mental harmony and the frustration of not being able to reach it completely.

My incessant moving around this planet from one country to another brought me personal and material satisfaction but left me with an empty feeling. Like a potted tree that hasn't yet found mother earth's ground in which to thrive. When I decided to come back to Canada five years ago, little did I know that it would be the beginning of a journey which would take me back in time and reunite me with my mother.

My sister had arranged for us to meet and although I wasn't too keen to do so, I accepted. I was tense, arrogant and disagreeable when we met. As my mother tried to kiss me I pulled back and simply offered my hand for a handshake. Her first words stayed engraved in my mind and heart for the days to come when she said, "All that I want is to ask if you could forgive me for not being the mother I wish I could have been, my son, I am so sorry..."

We met again a few days later and we talked openly about our pains, hurts, sorrows and expectations. It was the first time I saw my mother as a woman and as a human being; not from a child's point of view. My father's untimely passing away at thirty two left a beautiful young widow of twenty six years old with four children, the youngest 25 days old to take care of, several cattle ranches and a retail business in a male- oriented society. Having only an aging father and a younger sister in Brazil, she was alone and against all odds, she succeeded in raising her family.

Compassion and understanding gave me the strength not only to forgive her, but to forgive myself for the senseless pain I inflicted myself and the guilt it carries with it. We became very close again, and slowly the whole family seemed to come closer and closer. I soon found out that forgiveness is a positive energy that spreads much quicker than I thought. I have nephews, nieces, and cousins that are now an integral positive part of my life.

A well documented site on this subject is "A Campaign for Forgiveness Research"* where I found some important examples cited here. Each time we witness an act of forgiveness, we marvel at its power to heal, to break a seemingly unending cycle of pain. Forgiveness is something virtually all americans aspire to. In a Gallup poll nationwide survey, 94% said it was important to forgive, but it is not something we frequently offer. (In the same survey, only 48% said they usually tried to forgive others.) Perhaps this is because forgiveness is something we don't fully understand, or we associate forgiveness with weakness.

Some view forgiveness as an almost saintly quality that blesses only the very special and most certainly cannot be learned. In fact, the opposite is true, forgiveness is a sign of strength.

A research conducted at the University of Wisconsin in 1997 indicates forgiveness can be taught, with positive results.

I told a co-workers of mine that if she wanted to find a healthier source of strength after her separation from an abusive husband, she must forgive him before she could find her own way to happiness.

"After what I have been through with that bastard? When hell freezes over..." was her answer.

I suggested she try the three affirmations below for a few weeks and see if she still felt the same way.

I am good, compassionate and I now have the strength to forgive. After two weeks of affirmations she told me that the most difficult thing was to think of him and all the bad incidents. The pain, despair and guilt would come back but she now understood that she wanted to be able to forgive and in her prayers she asked God to help her to forgive.

I deserve to be happy and successful.
I am now ready to receive more love, support and wealth from the vast supply of the universe.
I knew then she had found her path.

Forgiving is not condoning; hurtful actions have consequences. Yet couples who communicate forgiveness may hold the key to stable marriages. What makes some marriages last a lifetime, while others falter and fall apart?

According to Professor Douglas Kelley of Arizona State University West, the key to long-term conjugal bliss may be in how well a couple communicates forgiveness. "These days the notion of equality, an eye for an eye, is prominent," says Kelley. "That makes forgiveness counter-intuitive - but at the same time, a lot of people who don't call themselves religious or spiritual are forgiving one another. Is it because they sense that they will reap the benefits of forgiving for years to come, or is there some other motive?"

In the end, Kelley hopes that embracing and communicating forgiveness can provide a sense of well-being and stability for couples living in an increasingly stressed society.

Forgiving doesn't change what has passed, neither does it justify or make it all right. It allows you to focus on your life from a pain free emotional state. The past no longer makes you cringe, cry or swear. Forgiveness simply helps you to let go of that negative baggage and makes a place for all the positive things you wish to have.

I know a lot of people who after a lover's break up or a friend's betrayal have vowed "I will never let anyone hurt me like that again." It is quite justifiable, it is your survival instinct, a protective shield taking over, but be careful that this shield will also prevent you from connecting with new people and eventually making new friends. This is negative living, and most people are not even aware of it. Forgiveness is letting go of that negative emotional baggage and starting on a new path stronger than before. It is very difficult, I know, to accept the fact that someone you loved and trusted, who has betrayed and stabbed you in the back, deserves your forgiveness.

When I lost a best friend of 25 years to what I thought was petty gossip, I was devastated and questioned the sincerity of her friendship all those years.

After forgiving her I can now look back and laugh at the good moments we had together. Sincerity is no longer a question, my love for her is the same, but I no longer need to see, speak or interact with her. Our roads just took different directions, that's all.

Make an assessment of the people in your life, and the ones who are gone. What are your feelings about them? Is there someone you feel "I dislike (or hate) that SOB" either for personal reasons or because of malicious gossip? Or is there someone you distanced from and in your book is unforgivable? You are carrying some heavy negative emotional baggage. Get rid of it AS SOON AS POSSIBLE if you want the good energy of positive living to reach you.

An important, well documented and proven factor is that your anger, hurt and pain not only will affect the way you communicate with others, but eventually will exclude you from social contact. Your self worth is constantly being questioned and if you don't take action it will eventually break down.

"Forgiveness allows one to overcome a situation that would otherwise be a major source of stress, both mentally and neurobiological. Forgiveness is thought to dramatically change the individual's biological homeostatic equilibrium. He will assess the neurobiological response associated with forgiveness and unforgiving-ness." Study of the Brain Functional Correlates of Forgiveness in Humans -Pietro Pietrini, M.D., Ph.D., Pisa - Italy.

Forgiveness benefits both, but you the most, because you left the negative baggage behind. You are now ready to receive the positive force, energy, love, wealth and success the universe has in store for you.

The other person doesn't even need to know, it is irrelevant. Neither do you have to bring that person into your life or closer circle any more. What matters is your thoughts and therefore your actions. If it is clean, clear and positive, so will your life, your friends and your future be.

"Forgiveness is both a decision and a real change in emotional experience. That change in emotion is related to better mental and physical health."

The weak can never forgive. Forgiveness is the attribute of the strong.

CHAPTER 9

HUMBLE YOURSELF OR LIFE WILL DO IT FOR YOU

HUMBLENESS

What is the meaning of "humble?" How is being "humble" expressed and is there a value to be found in it? Humble is the root word for "humility."

The meaning of "humility" is: The quality of being modest and respectful. Humility, in various interpretations, is widely seen as a virtue in many religious and philosophical traditions, being connected with notions of not having an ego. This is the meaning given by Wikipedia.

Remain humble in high positions because with position comes opposition. It's not going to be easy to reach the top and it's not going to be easy to stay there. Your character has to be right you have to watch how you handle power. If God gives you position you have to be careful not to abuse your power. You have to watch how you treat people beneath because if you don't you might find yourself brought back down to their level. You have to know how to act when God exalts you. There is no stage in your life that you cannot still be a student. You don't know everything and you never will. Until you can humble yourselves you not ready for success. You cannot be an effective leader if you cannot admit when you are wrong or listen to reason. You must be able to be corrected. Psalms 55:19 say's God will give ear and humble them, he who is enthroned from of old, Selah because they do not change and do not fear God. You do want God to have to humble you.

There are two types of people in the world the ones who think too much of themselves or the ones who think too little. Humility does not mean not knowing how good you are its means not announcing it all the time and acting like you are more important than everyone else. Let your work speak for you. Everyone has his or her job and the CEO can't operate without the janitor. We are all equally important in our respective lanes. Yes you may work hard but if you believe that you got to the top by yourself you are mistaken.

Often time's people who are doing something great and find themselves put in a leadership position feel the need to defend themselves. If you are doing something great you will have haters it's a given but no one should be able to put you in your feelings. There is a saying one monkey don't stop no show. Just because you have a few naysayers doesn't mean you are going to fail. No one can stop God from giving you what he wants you to have. Haters do not even need to be addressed because their opinion doesn't matter and you taking time out to check them makes them more important than they should be. Haters are going to get their fifteen minutes of fame but not on my time because I'm to focused on getting what God has for me to take time out of my busy schedule to address them. Colossians 4:5-6 say's 5 Walk in wisdom toward them that are without, redeeming the time. 6 Let your speech be always with grace, seasoned with salt, that ye may know how ye ought to answer every man. Silence is golden everyone doesn't deserve a reply. Sometimes when you reply to nonsense you cause yourself to sin. If you are more worried about someone else and what they have to say you are not focused enough. You should be so focused on God that you couldn't see a hater if they were standing right in front of you. TD Jakes said new levels bring new devils.

STAYING HUMBLE

Being humble and kind will make your life easier. It will help you do better at work and at home. Too much confidence will make you seem like a real pain in the ass. It's okay to admit that you are wrong about something and, more importantly, it's alright to concede that to others. This shows only one thing that you not only value your opinion and decisions, but that you also value the opinions and decisions of those around you.

Humble people are better able to cope with anxiety. They tend to find a useful perspective in life and how it should be lived. When it's not all about you, it is easy to contemplate and reflect because it is not always about you. Aside from that, humble people are more helpful than those who are conceited. Kindness is often overlooked as a sign of weakness but still can go a long way. Being kind can also make you happier. It feels good to be nice and help others and it can physically make you feel happier.

Stress, deadlines, and surprises can can drain people mentally and emotionally. Even the strongest of people can succumb to the power of unpredictability. Figuring out how to stay calm will make your life a lot more enjoyable, will make you more likable and make others think that you are more in control than you actually are. You can't control everything that happens to you, but you can control how you handle situations in a way that will have people gravitate toward you.

No matter what happens, always try to remain calm and humble. Everyone you've ever met is trying to do the same thing you do. Life is a lot easier when you accept that the world doesn't revolve around you only. No matter how independent you are, at the end of the day you will need someone to turn to especially your family. You will be surprised how relaxing and therapeutic that would feel.

No matter influential you are, how much money you have, how big your house is, our graves will always be the same size. So, stay humble.Yet, being humble doesn't necessarily mean talking down about one's self, or rejecting praise, or allowing people to walk all over us. This is more about establishing confidence and rapport, open-mindedness, and willingness.

Don't let yourself become intimidated by failure or success. Some of us are scared to make it because of the pressure our new position will entail. Do not buckle under pressure remain humble and work hard. Never put yourself so high on a pedestal that when something happens and you are knocked down a peg you give up. This isn't the first time you have failed and it won't be the last but the test is are you going to get up? God needs resilient people. If you have given up now at this level and resorted back to which you use to be, there is no way you were going to be able to handle where God was trying to take you. Don't be afraid of failure it makes you stronger as long as you don't let it keep you down. Trust in what God is doing in your life.

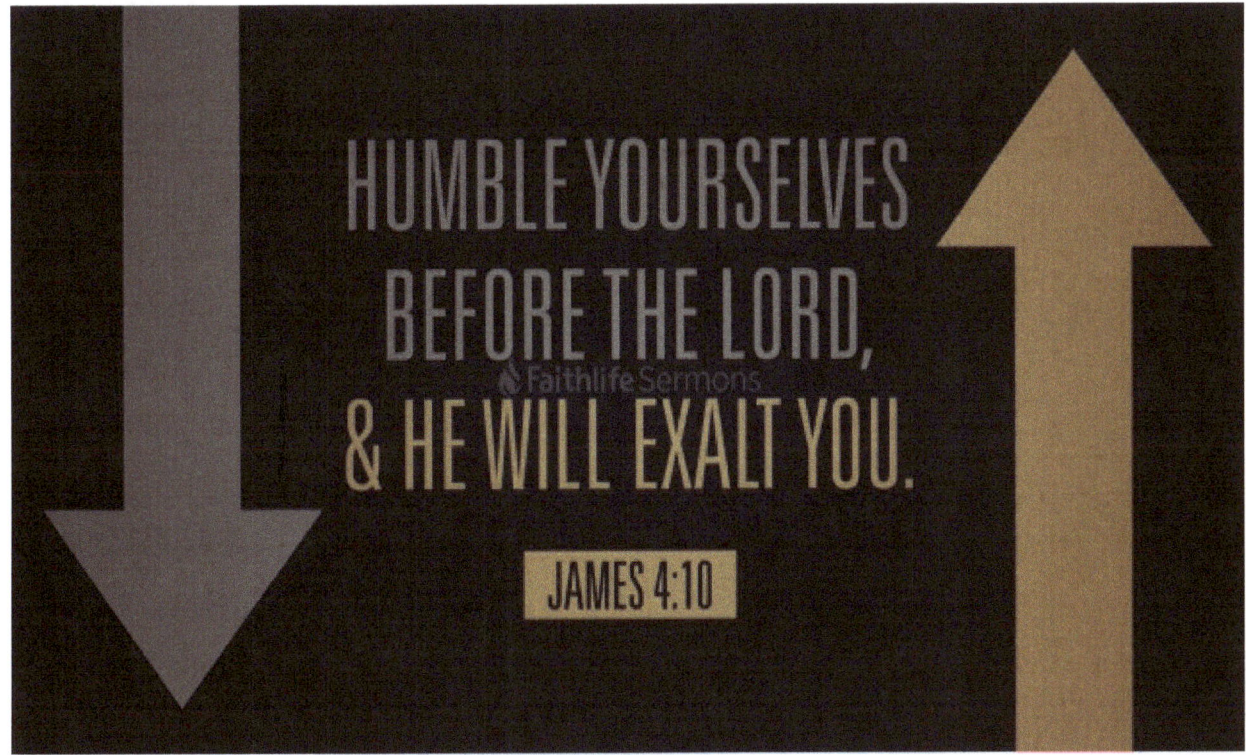

When you are truly winning people who don't even like you will testify to it.

Remember: "Success is not measured by what you accomplish, but by the opposition you have encountered, and the courage with which you have maintained the struggle against overwhelming odds.

This is saying it's not where you're at or where you're going it's where you've been and how you got here.

Matthew 23:12 And whoever exalts himself will be humbled, and he who humbles himself will be exalted.

CHAPTER 10

PRAYER

"If we provide food for the body which is perishable, than surely, it is our primary duty to provide food for the soul which is imperishable and such sustenance is found in Prayer." --**M.K. Gundi**

This is saying it's not where you're at or where you're going it's where you've been and how you got here.

Prayer is the very soul and essence of the religion, and, therefore, prayer must be the very core of the life of man, for no man can live without religion. There are some people in the world who, in the egotism of their reason, declare that they have nothing to do with religion. But it is like a man saying that he breaths, but that he has no nose.

Whether by reason, or by instinct, or by superstition, man acknowledges some sort of relationship with the Divine. Prayer is the very core of man's life, as it is the most vital part of religion. But prayer is no mere exercise of words or of the ears, it is no mere repetition of empty formula. Any amount of repetition of Rama name is futile if it fails to stir the soul. It is better in prayer to have a heart without words than words without a heart. It must be in clear response to the spirit which hungers for it. And even as a hungry man relishes a hearty meal, a hungry soul will relish a heartfelt prayer.

"He, who has experienced the magic of prayer, may do without food for days together, but not a single moment without prayer." "There is no inward peace without prayer." There is an eternal struggle raging in man's breast between the powers of darkness and of light, and he who has not the sheet-anchor of prayer to rely upon will be a victim to the powers of darkness. The man of prayer will be at peace with himself and with the whole world; the man who goes about the affairs of the world without a prayerful heart will be miserable and will make the world also miserable.

Begin, therefore, your day with prayer, and make it so soulful that it may remain with you until the evening. Close, the day with prayer so that you may have a peaceful night free from dreams and nightmares. Do not worry about the form of prayer. Let it be any form, it should be such as can put us into communication with the Divine. Only, whatever be the form, let not the spirit wander while the words of prayer run on out of your mouth.

"There is no peace without the grace of God, and there is no grace of God without prayer. That is why I ask you all to observe the habit of prayer. Prayer should proceed from the heart."

"Payer is the key of the morning and the bolt of the evening."

All things in the universe, including the Sun, the Moon and the Stars, obey certain laws. Without the restraining influence of these laws, the world would not go on for a single moment. You will go to pieces if you do not impose on yourselves some sort of discipline, and prayer is a necessary spiritual discipline.

"Heartfelt prayer steadies one's nerves, humbles one and clearly shows one the next step."

There will be darkness, disappointment and even worse; but we must have courage enough to battle against all there and not succumb to cowardice. There is no such thing as retreat for a man of prayer.

Worshipping God is singing the praise of God. Prayer is confession of one's unworthiness and weakness. God has a thousand names, some call Him Rama, some Krishna, others call Him Rahim and yet some call Him God. All worship the same spirit; but as all food do not agree with all, all names do not appeal to all. Worship of prayer is not being performed with the lips, but with the heart. And that is why it can be performed equally by the dumb and the stammerer. Rama was not only on the lips of Hanuman, He was enthroned in his heart.

We can never know if a prayer has or has not yielded the desired result. Prayer is never fruitless, but we cannot know what the fruit of it is.

When a man is down, he prays to God to lift him up. No, God needs no reminder. He is within everyone. Nothing happens without his permission. It is a reminder to ourselves that we are helpless without his support.

CONCLUSION

Living a happy, lively and positive life is fantastic, and is also good for your health. Being happy protects you from the stresses of life. We need stress in our lives to function properly, but high levels of stress are very unhealthy. Stress is linked to some of the top causes of death like heart disease, cancer and stroke. Be happy live longer, that's the best idea.

It was once said "The only thing in life that will always remain the same is change", I feel we have a duty to ourselves to change, for from change we develop and grow, we all have inside of us the power to make all necessary changes if we want to.

Even if we find ourselves in an intolerable situation we can always find comfort in the fact that our present situation will change if we apply ourself to make the necessary change in our lives.

Social networks groups and personal relationships are essential to our happiness and development. People are different, accept people for who or what they are, do not judge, avoid conflict and arguments.

Let go of all kinds of resentments and grudges. If an argument is unavoidable still try and make ever effort to understand the other persons situation and you could still find the argument dissolves and you just get along.

Increasing happiness is a great way to make your life more wonderfully joyous and could even lead to better health. Being happy is really easy, you just decide to be a happy person, think happy thoughts and do happy things. The choice is simple really, choose to be **Happy.**

Remember we're living in our **DASH**. We only live once so do your best to live a happy, healthy life. A life that will last long after you're gone.

Here are ways by which you can do this.

Being **grateful** is a great attitude. We have so much to be thankful for. Thank the taxi driver for bringing you home safely, thank the chef for a wonderful dinner and thank the guy who cleans your windows. Be grateful for all the small things and the big things in your life, be grateful for everything, live a life with an attitude of gratitude. Thank God daily for being alive.

Laugh and laugh heartily everyday. Heard a good joke? Tell your friends or family about it. As they also say -'Laughter is the best medicine'.

News is stressful. **Get less of it**. Some people just can't start their day without their daily dose of news. Think about it! When do you hear Good news reported, not often. 99% of news reported in the media, is bad news. Starting the day with bad news does not seem to be a sensible thing to do, in fact you don't need it, live a news free life. No news is good news! Convey your feelings, affections, friendship and passion to people you know. They will most likely reciprocate your actions. It is best not to keep pent up anger or frustrations, these are bad for your health. Instead of letting your emotions build up, find ways of expressing them in ways that will not cause more injury or hurt to anyone especially yourself.

Working hard brings tremendous satisfaction. It gives a feeling of being competent in finishing our tasks. Achievements are necessary for all of us, they give us a sense of value. Work on things that you feel worthy of your time. Always remember though, not to over work, don't let work take over your life, and reward yourself for the great things you achieve each day.

Learning is a joyful exercise. Try and learn something new everyday. read books, watch or listen to educational materials.

Learning expands and broadens our horizons, and also gives us more opportunities in the future.

Run, jog, walk, go swimming or even take up a sport. Do the things that makes your body feel alive. Do the things your body was made for. Feel alive, be alive. Most important, be a great example for others to pattern their life as yours.

Most people are about as happy as they make up their minds up to be. Remember, This is your DASH, you only live once. Why not be happy and leave an everlasting legacy on all you have came in contact with. Live **a great**;

DASH.....

The front cover of this book shows the sunrise, which represents the day you were born. The back inside cover is the sunset, representing you no longer living on this earth. The pages in between the covers represents your **DASH**. In other words your **LIFE.....**

THIS IS NOT LIVING!!!!!!!!!

STOP LIVING LIKE THIS!

DASH

There are many famous people that have died. Such as: Singers, actors, dancers, authors, athletes, rappers etc. If you were asked when where they born or died. Most of us wouldn't know either. What is known is how great they where at their craft. Their graves have their date of birth and date of death. Now think what's between those two dates? It's a DASH, separating those two dates. It's a small but actually a big symbol of that person's life. We are all living in our DASH right now. We know our date of birth but don't know when we're going to depart this life. You can have an effect on peoples life's, by becoming someone who inspires, motivate and help others. Just know how you live your life (Your DASH) now, will determine your legacy. Or how you will be remembered. Make the best of this life (DASH) you've been given and you to can leave something of meaning, that will live long after you have left this life.

Do not go yet; One last thing to do

If you enjoyed this book or found it useful I'd be very grateful if you'd post a short review on Amazon. Your support really does make a difference and I read all the reviews personally so I can get your feedback and make this book even better.

Thanks again for your support!

www.ingramcontent.com/pod-product-compliance
Lightning Source LLC
Chambersburg PA
CBHW061147010526
44118CB00026B/2898